Goudeau Gumbo For The Soul
A Literary Feast of Inspirational Poetry

Jacqui Hill Goudeau

Copyright © 2013 Jacquelyn Hill Goudeau

All rights reserved. No part of this publication may be reproduced, stored in a retrieval system, or transmitted in any form by means electronic, mechanical, photocopying, recording or otherwise, except the inclusion of brief quotations in a review, without prior permission in writing from the publisher.

ISBN-13: 978-0989623308

DEDICATION

To

El Shaddai
(Almighty God) the Original Poet

TABLE OF CONTENTS
"Ingredients"

Appetizer

✝	A Vessel Fit For Use	9
✝	I Will Lift Up My Eyes	10
✝	Well Done	11
✝	Steal Away	12
✝	Holding Onto The Master's Hand	13
✝	Outstretched Hands	15
✝	Which Side Are You On?	17
✝	I'm Dying To Make It In	19
✝	If The Righteous Scarcely Be Saved	20
✝	If I Be Lifted Up	21
✝	He Saved My Life	22
✝	Lord Change Me	23
✝	The Lord Nudged Me	24
✝	The Solid Rock	25
✝	My Court Case	26
✝	My Postmaster	28
✝	Bended Knees	30
✝	Who Was That Standing By You?	31
✝	Be Still And Know	33
✝	Never Alone	34
✝	What is Christmas All About?	36
✝	Thank God Someone Loves Me	38

✝	What Is Easter To You?	39
✝	My Walk With Jesus	41
✝	God's Treasure Chest	43
✝	No More I	44
✝	Jesus Came Down Low Enough For Me	45
✝	Just My God and Me!	47
✝	Thank God For The Valleys	48
✝	A Sure Foundation	50
✝	Together	51
✝	My Big Dream	52
✝	No Chance to Live	54
✝	Dare to Be a Priest Like Me	56
✝	But God!	57
✝	Sunday's On The Way	58
	Extra: Gumbo Recipe!	59
	About Author	63

~APPETIZER~

Few things in life are as comforting as food!

We use food to celebrate the good times as well as to help soothe the bad. We put a lot of time and thought into the simple question: "What do you want to eat?" Our appetite can easily be swayed based on our mood or surroundings.

Poetry is much like food. How many times have you stood in card aisles for long periods of time to pick the perfect card for a family member, co-worker or friend? It has to say the right thing! Whether humorous or serious, religious or practical, just like our food, there is an appetite that needs to be satisfied.

Goudeau Gumbo for The Soul - A Literary Feast of Inspirational Poetry is filled with various ingredients to meet your literary appetite. The poetry comes from all kinds of ideas, thoughts, life experiences and flavors, a kind of "gumbo of prose". Though written by the same poet, the lifestyle and heart of each person reading them brings a new and fresh taste to each one. We encourage you to journey with an open mind, not afraid to try something different! Sample the poetry in this book open to a different thought, a different mindset but a similar result…comfort.

Grab a warm cup of tea, or whatever makes you happy! We hope your heart will be touched and hopefully changed by the poetry in this book. Expect a word to comfort you on a difficult day, correct you on a challenging day, and make you laugh just when you need to. You may even spark a tear as you think on God's amazing grace and His provision for us all.

Whet your appetite and enjoy!

Jacqui G

"A Vessel Fit For Use"

Lord, I want to be, a vessel fit for use,

That You can call on any time, in any way You choose.

A vessel that's not dirty, in the world and filled with sin,

But a vessel that's so clean, others can look and see You in.

Lord I don't want to be stained with attitudes of a past life,

Not filled with self-righteousness, envy nor with strife.

But Lord, I want to be clean, shiny bright like new,

So others can see the difference in a vessel used by You.

Lord don't let me be broken because of things that people say,

Cause a vessel that gets used, sometimes gets knocked around each day.

But Lord I want to be made whole, not even a chip or two,

So others can see the completeness I have, since I gave my life to You.

Lord I don't want to be weak, nor do I want to bend,

But I want to be strong in You, so I can endure until the end.

And Lord there is another thing in You I want to be,

And that is an original, not paper, plastic or phony.

I don't want to just appear to be a vessel that's from You,

For when water, winds and fire comes, I want to make it through.

So since You are the Potter, and Lord, I am the clay,

Only You can make me what I'll be from day to day.

Lord, after You mold me and make me like You choose,

Then and only then will I be a vessel fit for use.

"If a man therefore purge himself of these, he shall be a vessel unto honor, sanctified and meet for the Master's use, and prepared unto every good work."
II Timothy 2:21

"I Will Lift Up My Eyes"

There comes a time in every saint's life,

When satan comes alone with trouble and strife.

We can't run to Mama, we can't go to Pop.

We have to lift up our eyes to the hills, to the top.

We look to the hills from whence cometh our help,

Because we know we can't make it alone by ourselves.

Since we wrestle not with flesh and blood,

All the physical strength wouldn't do any good.

We should be strong in the Lord, and the power of His might.

Only the good fight of faith we are told to fight.

With the breastplate of righteousness and our feet shod,

And the Sword of the Spirit, the Word of God.

To quench the fiery darts, we have faith for a shield,

Our loins gird with faith and we are off to the field.

Then just put your hand in the Unchanging Hand,

And having done all, He said to 'just stand'.

I can do all through Christ that strengthens me,

Cause the just live by faith, not what we can see.

You did what you're told and all is said and done,

Sit back in faith because your battle is won!

Since we know, we can't do it alone by ourselves,

We must lift up our eyes to the hills, from whence cometh our help,

Our help cometh from the Lord!

I will lift up my eyes to the hills-- From whence comes my help!
Psalms 121:1

"Well Done"

I must run the race before me, as the Bible tells me to,

I don't have my eyes on mankind, I don't have my eyes on you.

But my eyes are on the finish line and I'm pressing for a prize,

My reward is up in heaven, in a throne room in the skies.

I will run this race in victory, I will run this race in love,

I will run this race determined to reach that throne room up above.

I will run past all confusion, I will run past all despair,

I will run through disappointments, and will run past all my care.

I will run past trees of anger and hills of iniquity,

I will run past roads of discouragement when people laugh at me.

I will run past roads of talk, gossip and disgrace,

I will run up to the throne room and see Him face to face.

When I press my way through storms and winds and the race is finally won,

I will stand before my Savior, as He smiles and says, **"Well Done."**

His Lord said to him, 'Well done, good and faithful servant; you were faithful over a few things, I will make you ruler over many things. Enter into the joy of your Lord.
Matthew 25: 21

"Steal Away"

Lord, when I am hurting and overcome by deep despair,

Oh how I need to steal away in the comforts of prayer,

For only in Your presence is there such total peace.

I can huddle in Your arms and feel Your love release.

Right there is where You will meet me with Your ever-loving care,

And there is where I'll find You when I seek for You in prayer.

Even in the valleys when my pathway seems to stop,

Oh how I need to steal away with You- on the mountaintop.

For even in the valleys, with You Oh Lord I soar,

Over mountains, over hilltops going higher ever more.

When I see a soul that is aching and it seems there is no repair,

Oh how I love to steal away in the promises of prayer.

For Lord You know my friend and all they're going through,

So in prayer I seek to turn this friend to the answer that is in You.

So if I seem to forget and I'm caught in deep despair,

Remind me Lord to steal away, with You Oh God in prayer.

But you, when you pray, go into your room, and when you have shut your door, pray to your Father who is in the secret place; and your Father who sees in secret will reward you openly.

Matthew 6:6

"Holding On To The Master's Hand"

I love to walk with Jesus, I love to hold His hand,
I love to pray and talk to Him as we walk through the land.
I love to keep my hand in His, the safest place to be,
And He often lets me know He too, loves holding hands with me.

At times we stop and cry because of the abominations in the land,
We rejoice when truth wins out, as we walk and hold hands.
One day as we were walking, my eyes began to roam,
I got my eyes off Jesus and off my heavenly home.

I saw things that pleased the eyes and my hand began to slip.
Not considering the rough ground I walked on or how easily I could trip.
As my feet began to follow my eyes, my hand slipped completely free,
But following my eyes I couldn't hear Jesus calling me.

I was out on my own, following my own way,
With no one to lead me through the land, I got stuck in mud and clay.
I wiggled and fought in the mess wanting so much to get free,
But the things I had gotten into held on tight, constantly pulling me.

I tried so hard and prayed so hard to get out of the clay,
Until I heard Jesus softly say, "I am still The Way".
When I lifted up my eyes, I saw my Savior coming near.
My blinded eyes began to focus and I could see everything clear.

I saw my hand was not in His and I had gone my own path,
I saw the mess I gotten in would require a spiritual bath.
I saw the familiar nail scarred hand as He reached and pulled me out.
I hung my head, but Jesus said, "You don't have the time to pout"

As He washed me and cleansed me, He renewed the right spirit within,
I felt the joy and purity as He took away my sins.
Once again we walk, talk and cry cause of the abominations in the land,
But this time I have a tighter hold, onto the Master's hand.

***And I give unto them eternal life; and they shall never perish,
neither shall any man pluck them out of My hand.
John 10:28***

"Outstretched Hands"

I was living in a world of sin, full of junk and grime.
A world of hatred and coldness, a world so full of crime.
That world was completely dark, no light was ever there.
People were walking in darkness, but it seemed that no one cared.

One day some of us saw something we'd never seen before.
A light, at the end of a road that shone bright around a door.
Behind the door was knocking, someone anxious to get in.
People around were fleeing, cause the light was showing their sin.

I still could hear the knocking as my hand reached for the door,
Friends of mine were laughing, but I didn't care anymore.
As I turned the knob and pulled the door towards me, it opened wide.
I saw the light and glory that was on the other side.

As my eyes adjusted and I looked deep within,
I felt the darkness lift and felt myself get rid of sin.
The feeling was really beautiful, but nothing was as grand,
Nothing could compare to seeing the pair of Outstretched Hands!

They seemed to be so loving, anxious to reach and hold.
They made me feel like I'd never sinned, like my bones were made of gold.
Behind those hands was Jesus, dressed in white and full of light.
The love that shone inside His eyes removed my fear and fright.

As I fell into those loving arms, my eyes filled up with tears.
I thought of all the wasted time; the days, the months, the years.
Yet, when I heard the knocking and opened up the door,
The love and peace caught hold of me, as it never had before.

If you are in a world of darkness that seems like no one cares,
Remember the knocking on the door and the feeling that I shared.
But most of all, remember the love and the light that was so grand,
And if you open up your door, you will see those Outstretched Hands.

"Behold I stand at the door and knock, If any man hear My voice and open the door; I will come in and sup with him and he with Me."
Revelations 3:20

"Which Side Are You On?"

There is a battle going on in this world of sin,
A battle if good and evil, and everyone's in.
From the richest family to the poorest man,
From the seas to the mountains, all over the land.
The captains are satan, and God's Only Son.
And we are the warriors, **WHICH SIDE ARE YOU ON?**

This battle is raging from our mouths to our minds,
It's a constant battle from which many are blind.
Many people are trying to play in between,
But there is no middle, only one boundary is seen.
So you're either for satan or God's Only Son,
There is no middle, **SO, WHICH SIDE ARE YOU ON?**

Jesus is saying, "All for Me on this side."
But people are wrapped up in ignorance and pride.
They think by not choosing they sneak in at the end.
But only winning soldiers, the true soldiers get in.
The loser is satan, the winner, God's Son.
Are you winning or losing? **WHICH SIDE ARE YOU ON?**

The battle cry has been made, He'll be here with a shout.
If you're straddling the fence then you'll be left out.
You're either on your way to heaven or on your way to hell.
You're either for Him or you're not, only you can tell.

It's satan or Jesus, God's Only Son.

But the choice is still yours, **WHICH SIDE ARE YOU ON?**

And if it seem evil unto you to serve the LORD, choose you this day whom ye will serve; whether the gods which your fathers served that were on the other side of the flood, or the gods of the Amorites, in whose land ye dwell: but as for me and my house, we will serve the LORD.
Joshua 24:15

"I'm Dying To Make It In"

Heaven is a place where no sin will enter in,

A place of beauty, a place of peace, where joy knows no end.

Not everyone who thinks they're good is going to see this place.

Not everyone who cries 'Lord, Lord' will ever see God's face.

Though trials come, with His help I'm determined to take it.

Because the Lord is on the other side, I'm dying to make it.

I'm dying to see Jesus, I'm dying to make it in.

I'm dying to self, I'm dying to pride I'm dying out to sin.

You may be dying to go to a party or dying for a bottle of gin,

But I'm dying to see Jesus, and I'm dying to make it in.

We have to die before we die in order to make it in.

We have to die to this world and we have to die to sin.

If we die daily, the Christ in us will increase,

The more we die, the more we find the sin in us will decrease.

After we die we are no longer bound to this world in any way.

We will be free, free to be caught up on that soon coming day.

By dying daily I get just a little freer from this place,

And I'm well on my way to heaven to see my Savior's face.

I'm not dying to see a movie or dying to go to the mall.

I'm not dying to see payday or dying to make a phone call.

I'm not dying to go to a party or dying for a bottle of gin,

I'm just dying to see Jesus, and I'm dying to make it in.

I protest by your rejoicing which I have in Christ Jesus our Lord,
I die daily.
1 Corinthians 15:31

"If The Righteous Scarcely Be Saved"

If the righteous shall scarcely make it in,

Then what about you and all of your sin?

The righteous are praying and seeking God's will.

The ungodly are wavering, they lie and they steal.

The righteous are fasting, they even shut in,

Then what about you and all of your sin?

The righteous lay hands and the sick recover.

While your cheating on your spouse and on your lover.

The righteous are suffering and really going through.

And you get upset if someone looks at you.

If the righteous shall scarcely make it in,

Then what about you and all of your sin?

The ungodly go to church and don't learn a thing,

They sing in the choir but don't know what they sing.

While the righteous bruise satan from one point to another,

The ungodly are fighting and killing their brother.

The righteous are willing to endure to the end,

But what about you and all of your sin?

One day from the sky the trumpet will sound.

The righteous are lifted and you're on the ground.

At the judgment the book of Life will be opened wide,

You look and see that righteous man on the other side.

You see through all his prayer and trials he scarcely made it in,

Now what about you and all of your sin?

"And if the righteous scarcely be saved, where shall the ungodly and sinner appear?" I Peter 4:18

"If I Be Lifted Up"

Jesus said, "If I be lifted up, I'll draw all men unto Me"
I'll pull them out and save them from the sinful raging sea.
If I be lifted up, I'll cleanse men's hearts within,
I will purge them with hyssop and remove them from their sins.
I'll wash them with My Word, and I'll overflow their cups,
I'll do all of this and more, if I be lifted up.
If I be lifted up, I'll draw all men unto Me,
I will loose the band of wickedness and set the oppressed free.
I will heal the broken hearted and their souls I'll satisfy.
I'll make them worthy of the kingdom, and all their tears, I'll dry.
I'll touch their blinded eyes and cause them to see.
If I be lifted up, I'll draw all men unto Me.
I'll put crowns on their heads and give them robes of righteousness.
Everything they put their hands to, I'll multiply and bless.
I'll continue to love them and answer when they call,
I'll be the strong arm beside them to catch them when they fall.
I'll give them new lives to live in holiness and love,
To live on earth until the day I call them from above.
I'll shower down blessings in their overflowing cups,
I'll do all of this and more, if I be lifted up.

And I, if I be lifted up from the earth, will draw all men unto Me.
John 12:32

"He Saved My Life"

I was alone in a world full of sin,

I was seeking and searching for life within.

I was alive to the world, but dead in my soul.

I had nothing to live for and nothing to hold.

My life was in shambles with troubles and strife,

But one day I met Jesus, and He saved my life.

I had problems, sickness; I had doubt and pain.

I thought I had everything, but I had nothing to gain.

To some I was living, but I was dying inside.

I was dying in sin, I was dying in pride.

I was offered booze, I was offered dope,

But I was dying and dying without any hope.

Then one day I met Jesus and He saved my life.

I was through with the shambles, troubles and strife.

I was through with the sickness the doubt and the pain,

I was through with the problems and had all to gain.

I have joy I have love I have peace from within,

I have life, I have hope and have cleansing from sin.

But most of all I have Jesus, to have and to hold.

The life He has given me is more precious than gold.

I love Him and thank Him for taking my strife,

He not only loved me, but He saved my life.

Neither is there salvation in any other:
For there is none other name under heaven given among men,
whereby we must be saved.   Acts 4:12

"Lord, Change Me"

So many times we look and see faults in one another,

Then we lift up our eyes and whisper, "Lord, change my brother"

You see how you didn't agree with all that he may do,

But have you ever stopped to think of how others may see you?

We're so quick to find the many ways others could be wrong,

Sometimes even knowing we do the same things all along.

But if we'd stop, look at ourselves and really try to see,

We would lift up our eyes and whisper, **"Lord Change Me."**

Change the things not like You, things I say and do.

Change my mind, change my heart and my motives too.

Change the way I see my brother and the life he may lead,

So I can look past what I see, and only see his need.

Help me be the man or woman you want me to be,

Lord I yield my all to You, Lord please change me!

When we reach the place we see ourselves and the mess were really in,

We'll see the motive of our hearts and see all of our sins.

We'll see were not perfected and not living all right,

We'll see we have many faults that show under the Light.

So when you look at your brother, trying to see what you can see,

Remember, then lift up your eyes and whisper, **"Lord Change Me!"**

And why do you look at the speck in your brother's eye, but do not perceive the plank in your own eye? Luke 6:41

"The Lord Nudged Me"

One day I saw an old man, sitting shivering in the street.

His clothes were old and ragged, he had no shoes on his feet.

His eyes were dark with circles, so much sorrow I could see

As I looked into his lonely eyes, that was when the Lord nudged me.

I was a little doubtful, but my heart was burdened down.

I couldn't walk by and leave that old man on the ground.

So I talked to that old man, then I took him out to eat.

I fed him, then clothed him and put new shoes on his feet.

All along I spoke of Jesus, I told him all about my Lord,

He listened very silently, but took in my every word.

At the end of the day, he wanted to be saved, a bit to my surprise;

Right then he repented and God saved him, with tears of joy in his eyes.

When I left that old man, he was smiling joyfully,

He said for the first time, he saw a picture of Jesus- in me.

The last time I saw that old man, they had put him in his grave,

I thanked God through tearful eyes that his soul at last was saved.

Now I rejoice to think of that old man, sitting in glory,

And I thank God that I responded, when the Lord nudged me.

But whoever has this world's goods, and sees his brother in need, and shuts up his heart from him, how does the love of God abide in him? 1 John 3:17

"The Solid Rock"

When we are in a storm, and the waves are Oh so high,
We are tossed to and fro, and we cannot see the sky.
We can't see the dry land and we cannot see the dock,
We look to see if we can find just one good solid rock.
We don't need a rock that wavers or a rock that wobbles some.
We don't need a rock that slips and slides with every wind that comes.
We sure don't need a little rock that will go beneath the waves,
We need a solid, grounded Rock that we know surely saves.
We need a Rock that been through every trial and every test,
Only one that's been around could hold out the best.
The Rock we need has got to stand above the waves and winds;
The Rock that we need in this storm must be high above our sins.
When we get a hold of this Rock and safely watch the storm,
We really don't see what on earth could have made us so alarmed.
The waves are like a tub that a baby's foot has kicked,
The winds are like a small balloon, a pin has gently pricked.
But if we'd tried to go through the storm without the Savior's help,
We would have drowned in defeat and could blame no one but ourselves.
But thank God we didn't try to swim just to reach the dock,
Instead we looked to Jesus, that one good Solid Rock!

And the rain descended, and the floods came, and the winds blew, and beat upon that house; and it fell not: for it was founded upon a rock.
Matthew 7:25

"My Court Case"

I always thought the murderer committed such great sin,
And the prostitute and drug addict, would never make it in.
It always seemed the drunkard and thief were really bad,
But I found out something else that really made me sad.

I found that I was deep in sin and authorities looked for me,
And I found that on my soul, the devil put out an APB!
I didn't have enough money and I knew that I was wrong,
I told myself that I was good, but was guilty all along.

I tried to hide in dark corners in the day and alleys late at night,
But everywhere I went I was exposed by a search light.
In my desperation, I sought Jesus a Lawyer and Friend,
He told me not to worry, but just turn myself in.

I couldn't see His planning, but I confessed anyway,
I ended in a small court where they heard my case one-day.
They put me on probation and soon I was free,
I had to stay in Jesus will, but that was fine with me.

I asked Jesus where He was when I was running wild,
He said "A place called Calvary, just for you My child."
After He finished the work He did at Calvary,
He said He went to the Highest Court to plead my case for me!

They told Him about my record, all my sins large and small.
He looked at my accusers and said, "I died for them one and all."

After He told me everything, the tears streamed down my face,
I thanked Him and praised Him for His amazing grace.
I dried my eyes and asked Him, "Lord what is Your fee?"
He smiled, looked at His nail scarred hands and said "My Child, this is on Me."

And not only so, but we also joy in God through our Lord Jesus Christ, by whom we have now received the atonement.
Romans 5:11

"My Postmaster"

Sometimes we as Christians receive mail of grief,
We get trials and tribulations all sent from a thief.
He comes to steal, kill and destroy,
He has no compassion on any girl or boy.

As you open your mail wondering if you will make it through,
Let me share something, a fact from me to you.
When you receive Jesus and live on Straight Street,
Jesus is your Postmaster, mail is laid at His feet.

He sifts it and tries it according to what you can bear,
It's nice to have a Postmaster that we know really cares!
When a package is too high for you to climb or too long to make it through,
Or if it's much too deep or just too wide for you.
The Postmaster won't put His stamp which means it can't be mailed,
Which in turn simply means the thief again has failed.
Sometimes the thief tries to be slick and mail it anyway,
That's when you need to live and know just what the Master says.

The Postmaster has written a book,He gave to you and me,
His Word lets us know just what packages will be.
He lets us know what isn't allowed what is not His will,
But some of us take it anyway and then send Him the bill!

But He paid it all at once, hanging on Mt. Calvary,

Which stopped a lot of the mail the thief sends you and me.

So when sickness, doubt and failure try to come your way,

And you open up the door that bright sunny day:

If the devil sends heart trouble but you know God is a heart mender,

You can look the devil in the eye and say "Return to sender"

Then rejoice and thank the Lord, and sing a joyous song,

Cause the package is back in the pit, just where it belongs!

There hath no temptation taken you but such as is common to man: but God is faithful, who will not suffer you to be tempted above that ye are able; but will with the temptation also make a way to escape, that ye may be able to bear it.

1 Corinthians 10:13

"Bended Knees"

If you've done wrong or if you are living in sin,

And you really want God to step right in.

Before you cry out "Lord forgive me please"

Humble yourself, get on your bended knees.

Say, Lord forgive me for all of my sin,

Fill me, help me, give me joy within.

Purge me and clean me and scrub out my mouth,

Separate me from sin like the north from the south.

If there is anything in me that is not like you Lord,

Reveal it to me with Your precious Word.

Then take it and toss it deep into the sea,

Never to be remembered by You or by me!

When you stand on your feet and start praising His name,

You will find that your life will never be the same.

Go tell someone what happened and tell of God's grace,

Tell how you prayed and sought for God's face.

Tell them how God came into your life,

Tell how He took all your trouble and strife.

And as you tell others how God heard your every plea,

Don't be ashamed to admit you were on bended knees.

Don't be too high to come down a little low,

He doesn't need you, you need Him, you know!

So before you cry out "Lord help me please,"

Humble yourself, get on your bended knees.

Yet regard the prayer of Your servant and his supplication, O Lord my God, and listen to the cry and the prayer which Your servant is praying before You today. 1 Kings 8:28

"Who Was That Standing By You?"

I saw you walking just the other day,

I saw you very clearly as you went on your way.

I know, no matter what anyone may say or do,

I know I saw a Man standing next to you.

A car was coming down the street at a tremendous speed,

That Man held up His hand, did you thank Him for that deed?

The way that car stopped instantly sure seemed really hard.

It is good that Man next to you was really on His guard.

Then one day I saw you, you were at the grocery store,

Your basket was full, your bank almost empty. You knew you needed more.

And I know no matter what anyone may say or do,

I know I saw that same Man, standing next to you.

As you reached inside your wallet to get what little you had,

I know I saw Him slip in more, I know that you were glad!

I even saw your children as they went out for the day,

And I know it was that same Man that followed them along the way.

Then that week that you were sick and stricken to your bed,

The doctors had all given up and said you'd soon be dead.

When I went to visit you late one-week night,

They said you would be asleep, but I know I saw a Light.

As I opened your bedroom door, I didn't know what to do!

Cause there was that same Man, praying next to you!

The room was lit in glory, light streaming through the place,

I squinted but could still see tears rolling down His face.

Soon you were healed and thanking God you were free,

Only then did I finally notice, He also followed me!

Very soon we will be caught up to meet Jesus in the sky,

And I know He will look familiar, but I may not realize why.

We will walk between the pearly gates headed for the throne,

And I know I will recognize the Light that in your room had shone.

And I know, without a doubt or what anyone may say or do,

We will walk in and see that same Man that stood by me and you!

Lo, I am with you always, even to the end of the age.
Matthew 28:20

"Be Still and Know"

We are in a world of progress where everyone is on the go,
But God is whispering softly **"Be still and know."**
We're off in the morning going on our way,
Not realizing God is waiting for thanks for another day.
At lunch time we are hungry and ready for a meal,
Not thanking God for our food, how bad the Lord must feel.
After lunch we cool down, but were still not going slow,
And God is still saying **"Be still and know."**
After work and through the traffic or wherever we may be,
We still have not thanked Him that our souls have been made free.
After a whole day, perhaps then we may stop and see;
We lift up our heads and say "Thanks for keeping me."
We didn't want to slow down progress and get left behind,
Yet it doesn't take a lot of time to thank Him in our minds.
We can thank God while working, while we are on the go,
That's why God is saying **"Be still and know."**
Be still and know God is with us as we go through the day,
Be still and know He hears you when you pause the day to pray.
Don't get too busy and not know God is there,
To know He is God, and has you in His care.
So when you wake in the morning before you get on the go,
Pause a while to listen, pray, and **be still and know.**

"Be still, and know that I am God: I will be exalted among the heathen" Psalms 46:10

"Never Alone"

One day I sat thinking alone in my room,
I was filled with self-pity, loneliness and gloom.
I didn't think anyone really cared for me,
Or knew of my battles, sorrows or needs.
While down in depression I began to groan,
Just by thinking how I was all alone.
No sooner had I allowed grief to set in,
I felt a sweet presence; like a soft summer's day wind.
And as I relaxed, I heard a voice say so clear,
You are never alone, because I am always near.
I didn't understand it, I saw no one there.
And no one really knew of the burdens I bear.
No one knew the loneliness the feeling of loss,
No one knew of the nights that I turned and tossed.
But the voice was consistent, pleading with me,
You are never alone, why can't you see.?
I am there through your stress, troubles and pain,
There through sunshine, sleet and through the rains.
I was there while you tossed and turned through the night,
I was there while you stood through the faithful fight.
You are never alone my child can't you see?
Wherever you go Someone's there, and it's Me!
Now I am no longer in pity, no longer in gloom,
Now I talk to my Lord when I am in my room.
He bears all my burdens and guides me in deed,
He's the all present comfort that I always need.

With this knowledge inside, I know I have grown,
Because God let me know, I am never alone!

"I will never leave thee, nor forsake thee."
Hebrews 13:5

What is Christmas All About?

Twas the evening of Christmas, such a beautiful night,
A manger is lit with a glorious light.
The animals are quiet, no one utters a word,
Only the praises of angels can softly be heard.
Many people have come, they've all gathered near,
Such joy in their hearts, and their eyes full of tears.
What is the reason for the joy felt within?
The Savior is born, the Redeemer from sin!
He is here to save us, so there's no need to fright,
The evening of Christmas what a beautiful night!

33 years after Christmas, on a hill far away,
Our Savior is crucified, what a mourningful day.
He is scourged He is spat on and unmercifully beat,
Nails are driven in His hands and in His feet.
The animals are silent, no one utters a word;
As He is pierced in the side by the edge of a sword.
The sky is black, dark clouds hang down low,
The ground is shaken the wind ceases to blow.
But three days after this, what a glorious morn!
Just as the day Jesus our Savior was born.
He is risen, alive and He's glorified!
Interceding for us on the Father's right side.
He is the Truth, the Life and the Way,

Three days after Calvary, what a glorious day!

One day from the sky will arise such a clatter!

A trumpet will sound and the clouds will all scatter.

And who to our expectant eyes will appear?

Jesus our Savior with a Joyous cheer!

And placing His foot gently upon the land,

He will call for His church, with outstretched hands.

We who know Him and are waiting, will go meet the Lord,

And the praises of saints will surely be heard!

If you're cleansed by His blood and redeemed from sin,

You can rest in His promise, He's coming again!

Christmas didn't end in Bethlehem that beautiful night;

Cause even now we are looking for that marvelous light.

Be ready and look for Him, He'll be here with a shout,

And you'll find just what Christmas is all about.

In parting with you I would just like to say,

Merry Christmas to you all, and hope to see you that day!

For unto us a Child is born, unto us a Son is given.
Isaiah 9:6

"I Thank God Someone Loves Me"

Many times I wander and go where I shouldn't go,

Thinking many times that no one will ever know.

I cause trouble for myself and added burdens to bear,

But I thank God someone loves me enough to kneel in prayer.

For just as I'm about to stumble or as I'm about to fall,

That prayer has reached my Father and I hear His loving call.

And then sometimes I'm hurt by what someone may have said,

I don't release and forgive, I internalize instead.

The bitterness starts to eat me up and I toss and turn at night,

But I thank God someone loves me enough to set me right.

For just as I'm about to give up and don't care how I live,

The word of God comes in and reminds me to forgive.

There are even times of wondering if someone loves me still,

Even though throughout my life I would lie, cheat and steal.

My life was so full of sin, and so many times I cried,

But I thank God Someone loves me enough to come and die.

Cause when I was without strength or light so I could see,

In due time because of my sin, Jesus died for me.

So I thank God Someone loves me and over many countless years,

He has broken bands of oppression and dried my many tears.

There will never be a greater love shown towards me or you,

I thank God Someone loves me, and my friend He loves you too!

For God so loved the world that He gave His only begotten Son, that whoever believes in Him should not perish but have everlasting life. John 3:16

"What Is Easter To You?"

Is it coloring Easter eggs bright orange, yellow and blue?

Is it Easter egg hunts or a bunny or two?

Is it going to church that one time every year?

It is buying nice clothes for the ones you love dear?

Is it hats, is it ties, is it flowers and bows?

Is the meaning forgotten, does anyone know?

Has the blood been forgotten have the scars been erased?

Now stories of Easter bunnies, my Lords been disgraced.

As my mind goes way back to that day long ago,

The memory of Easter, the real story I know.

As my Lord was convicted and unjustly tried,

For your soul and my soul He willingly died.

But thank God today that my soul He has cleansed,

He has loved me, and kept me and forgiven my sins.

I thank Him, I love Him for the blood He has shed,

For without my Jesus, my soul would be dead.

On the third day He rose with the keys in His hand,

With the victory completely, my Lord is so grand!

Since He has the keys to death, hell and the grave,

Now we who He died for can surely be saved.

To me Easters the victory, the joy and the love,

To me it's the Gift that God sent from above.

To me it's the blood on the cross that He shed,

To me it's the raising of Christ from the dead.

To me it's the knowledge of God's love for me,

To me it's just knowing He set my soul free.

If you still think Easter is eggs and fine clothes,
You need to be talking to someone who knows!
So let's send our minds to that day long ago,
The memory of Easter, the real story we know.

***He is not here, but is risen: remember how He spoke unto you
when He was yet in Galilee,
Luke 24:6***

"My Walk With Jesus"

A path of destruction I did walk,
Full of sinful desires and evil talk.
A path covered with blood of sinners now dead,
A path full of doubt, hatred, coldness and dread.
This path did I tire and no longer want to go,
I knew something was missing, but what? I didn't know.
One day as I walked on this path of woe,
Another path I did see, and thought I would go.
Many times I had passed it but not once did I try,
This time I decided to, but don't ask me why.
I started this path towards what I didn't know,
But the warmth and the love that I felt made me go.
Lots of talk of the bible I did hear on this path,
A choice of eternal life or of seeing God's wrath.
These words I did hear when I was a child,
But so full of the world, I did take those words mild.
From another perspective inside I did see,
From outside "they're crazy" But inside "They love me"
As I walked on this path many things I did learn,
For the evil of the world, I no longer yearned.
Because Jesus loves me, with Him I will go,
Wherever He leads me- I love Him you know.
For He loved me first and He died on the cross,
A Savior I've gained, some friends I have lost.
Once as I walked this path; quite narrow you see,
Old satan came along and tried to mess with me.

At first I did weaken and I thought I would fall,
But using my faith, on Jesus name I did call.
We He didn't come quickly, my faith I lost some,
I was really upset, because He didn't come.
As my foot slipped beneath me and I started to fall,
A spark of my faith lit, and boy did I call!
And just when I thought my cries were in vain,
A hand at my elbow, lifted me up again!
"Jesus where were You" I asked in relief!
I was right here behind you, waiting on your belief.
I thank God today the path of woe, I did leave,
You too can walk here if you only believe.
For satan is sly and he really hates me,
But I serve a God far much greater than he.
So while you are walking on this path my friend,
Believe Jesus is behind you, all the way to the end.

The steps of a good man are ordered by the LORD: and he delights in his way.
Psalms 37:3

"God's Treasure Chest"

I openly display my treasures,
The things that are precious to me.
I do not put them behind concrete walls,
Bound by lock and key.
I display them with grace and with pleasure,
So the whole wide world can see.
The treasures I have in this vessel,
Are the gifts that God has given to me.
We shouldn't seek for earthly treasures,
The things that can rip and break.
Things that are eaten with moth or rust,
Or thieves can break in and take.
We should earnestly seek for the treasures,
So priceless no money can buy.
These treasures are gifts of the spirit,
They can't be purchased though many may try.
If you want to have precious treasures,
You must invest your life wisely.
You must lay up treasures in heaven,
Where Jesus is the door, faith the key.
Your life must be lived for His glory,
You must seek always to give Him your best.
Then you will find your life precious and valuable,
And find you are in God's treasure chest!

But we have this treasure in earthen vessels, that the Excellency of the power may be of God, and not of us. 2 Corinthians 4:7

"No More I"

When you saw me running the streets and living deep in sin,
That was the outward reflection of the evil that was within.
Although I thought, I was okay and living pretty good,
Sin was there and deep inside I was not doing what I should.
It used to be about me and what I wanted to do,
It was what I wanted to believe and what I already knew.
It wasn't always what can I do for you but what could you do for me,
It wasn't what was expected of me, but it was what I wanted to be.
Even though I didn't follow crowds, I still had my own sins,
And the way I was on the outside, just reflected the evil within.
But then that day when Jesus came and shone His glorious light,
He brightened up the dark spots and made my wrong paths right.
It's no more what I want, but what God wants me to do.
It's no more what I want to believe, but what God tells me to.
It's no more what can God do for me, but here I am- send me,
It's no more what I want to do but what God expects from me
I still don't follow the crowds, because Jesus is my way,
He's the one I strive to follow as I live from day to day.
So do you see the difference from when I was living a lie?
It's living for God now, it's simply "No More I'
Don't think it's me that's living a life of love and free from sin,
Because it is "No More I" but the Christ that lies within!

I have been crucified with Christ; it is no longer I who live, but Christ lives in me; and the life which I now live in the flesh I live by faith in the Son of God, who loved me and gave Himself for me. Galatians 2:20

"Jesus Came Down Low Enough for Me"

When I was still a sinner, I was all but free,
But Jesus found the time to come down here and visit me.
He told me with His loving word, He is the only way,
And by listening and believing, I know I am saved today!

When I tried to figure out the way, I couldn't understand,
Jesus found the time to come down here and hold my hand.
He led me and He guided me, opened doors I could not see,
Of all the people in the world, He took time to come lead me!

When I hit a dark spot and I couldn't see one day,
Jesus sent light low enough to help me along the way.
When I fell into temptation or went where I shouldn't be,
Jesus had the love and grace to forgive, even me!

When I needed keeping power and strength to hold on tight,
He said He would give me power, He said He would, not might.
Of all the people in this world, much higher than me,
Jesus sent His spirit low enough one day to land on me!

When my body and my health wasn't all that it should be,
Jesus took the pain and stripes to restore my health to me.
When accidents and hazards tried to come my way,
Jesus let His blood run low enough to cover me all day.

Of all the people in the world who He could go and see,

Jesus came down low enough to come and set me free!

So if you think that you are too low for Jesus Christ to see

Remember, He came low enough one day to save me.

This is a faithful saying, and worthy of all acceptation, that Christ Jesus came into the world to save sinners; of whom I am chief.
1 Titus 1:15

"Just My God and Me"

Though I may not follow the crowd at times,
And it may seem I am not having fun.
And I may seem very quiet at times,
Like I'm running this race alone.
Don't worry about me because my soul is free,
And my times all alone is just my God and me!

If you hear me at night and I'm trying,
To hold out and not start to crying.
If you think I am lonely and sad,
Don't worry because my soul is glad.
I could just be thinking of Calvary,
Whatever, don't worry it's my God and me!

If I'm sitting alone and smiling; don't think I am insane,
The rivers that flow in my belly are probably moving again.
If I throw up my hands in a praise,
I'm just doing just what the word says.
So if I'm rejoicing and dancing with glee,
I'm not dancing alone; it's just my God and me!

Oh, magnify the Lord with me, and let us exalt His name together. Psalm 34:3

"Thank God for the Valleys"

I was standing in a valley walking on an endless road,
Headed for the mountain, carrying my usual load.
I walked very slowly; so I wouldn't tire quick,
On my back a giant bundle, in my hand, a walking stick.

As I walked through the valley; headed for the mountain base,
I felt myself grow weary, even at my slow pace.
So I stopped to examine the large load upon my back,
So many things I couldn't believe I took the time to pack.

I began to throw away all the things that hindered me,
Many things that were hidden there I had never even seen.
All the sins and weights that so long had held me down,
I felt the freedom come as I threw them to the ground.

Then I picked up my stick and began my walk again,
Feeling the weight lifted cause I set aside my sin.
I climbed the mountain with patience; forgetting all that was behind,
I pressed and fought the hardships with a clearly made up mind.

Finally as I reached the top and felt the victory!
I turned and looked how far I'd come with my Savior guiding me.
That valley seemed at one time to be such a trial to me,
When all along my sins were all that hindered me.

I thank God for that valley, where a victory was won,
I realized not just how low I was, but learned how far I'd come.

I look ahead and see higher mountains that I must climb,

But I'm deeply inspired by the victory I left behind.

So as I turn towards my new goal, I smile then I stop,

To take a deep breath of victory, upon the mountain top.

Therefore we also, since we are surrounded by so great a cloud of witnesses, let us lay aside every weight, and the sin which so easily ensnares us, and let us run with endurance the race that is set before us. Hebrews 12:1

A Sure Foundation

What makes a woman reach out to another?
What makes a man so concerned for his brother?
What would cause one to think past their own life?
To seek how to help someone else through their strife

It takes a person who is mature, confident and sure,
Who knows that their input will lend to a cure.
One person may travel and touch every nation,
Another may give to a worthy foundation.

Someone may offer a home to a family in need,
Another may find someone on the street to feed.
Through touching our children and helping them soar,
We're teaching them to believe God for so much more.

But one thing is sure it takes all of us,
To build our community with love and with trust.
It takes someone with vision to reach this generation,
It takes people like you, who can turn this whole nation.

It has never been the call for just one man to hear,
But it takes every day calls to each of us, every year.
Don't ever think that you're serving in vain,
Everything you do, adds to another child's gain.

Some plant, others water, and increase is near;
You have planted in lives that is why you are here.
Keep reaching and touching this next generation,
Cause your efforts are building a sure, firm foundation.

According to the grace of God which was given to me, as a wise master builder I have laid the foundation, and another builds on it. But let each one take heed how he builds on it.

1 Corinthians 3:10

"Together"

Together with joys. Together with pains.
Together thru storms. Together thru rains.

Together with laughter, thru sorrows and trials.
Together thru years of changing lifestyles.

Together we are and together we'll be.
Together just you, just God and just me.

Together we'll cope. Together we'll pray.
Together we'll make it thru each lasting day.

Together we'll walk. Together we'll stand.
Together we'll cry and hold on hand in hand.

Together is you, together is me.
Together is God and together we'll be!

"What therefore God hath joined together, let not man put asunder."

Mark 10:9

My Big Dream

One day I was sleeping, alone in my bed,

When visions and dreams danced hard in my head.

I thought I could touch them since they were so real,

Those dreams were so vivid, they could talk, they could feel.

In one dream I was of singing, and praising God's name,

My songs so anointed, I could not take the fame.

Another dream was of writing one book after another,

One dream was to finance a home for my brother.

I dreamed I could reach men and women behind bars,

I even dreamed I was helping by simply selling cars.

I dreamed I built a home for unwed mothers,

I dreamed I was counseling and helping others.

In one part of my dream I was on a talk show,

Another part showed me with children in tow.

But the one thing that was consistent in one dream or another,

I was always found helping and encouraging others.

My big dream is to touch people, from every nation and tongue,

My big dream is to have lots of money so I can help someone .

My big dream is to serve God in any way that I can,

My big dream is to be able to hold out my hand.

When I woke from my state of dreaming that day,

I was a bit confused, but I heard the Lord say.

I gave you those dreams and you must be a success,

I have called you to go forward, multiply and to bless.

I have gifted you to make money to further My goals,

I have called you so you can touch many souls.

I stood ready to work, because now I understood,

By working my dream, I will help change the world for good.

For a dream comes through much activity, and a fool's voice is known by his many words.
Ecclesiastes 5:3

"No Chance to Live"

When you're young in this world, there so much to do,

So many indulgences the world offers you.

There is plenty running the streets during the day,

There are movies and dances, places to go and to play.

You feel there's no time for church and no time to give,

You feel if you turn to Christ, you will have no chance to live.

You feel you are much too young to live for the Lord,

All those prayers and church you say make you bored.

Yet you see different friends your age who have died,

They've tried many things, but Christ they've not tried.

But still no time for Christ, and no time to give,

Cause you don't want to pass up your chance to live!

As you get older and mature quite a bit,

You are now seeking money! You want all you can get!

All of your schooling for things you must know,

So much to learn, many places to go.

You say Jesus can wait, and when you get, then you will give,

You say right now you are just beginning to live!

You say you don't have time to sit on a pew,

While so many opportunities are presented to you.

So you press and reach to meet all your goals,

On the way you see people dying and losing their souls.

They passed up a chance for Jesus, a chance to give,

But you continue to pursue, your chance to live.

Then you are much older, your goals are mostly met,

You retire to live comfortably; you feel you are all set.

You started a family many years ago,

You had the chance to help them and watch them grow.
No more working; But money is still coming in,
You've got money to blow and money to lend!
You go to church occasionally and occasionally give,
Cause this is a brand new life, a new chance to live!
There is going to dinners, visiting friends old and new,
You feel you have it all but still no repentance from you.
All the things you couldn't do, all the years before,
You are going to do them and a whole lot more!
But there was one appointment with death you didn't plan to make,
That appointment you kept, and your life he did take.
Before judgment you say "I was going to go to church, and I planned to give,
I was going to accept you Jesus after I had my chance to live"
"What does if profit a man to gain the world and lose his soul?
What good did all your money do, or meeting all your goals?
Ever since you were young, I constantly called you,
But you chose the things of the world, things you wanted to do.
You may have been young or old, but you still had a choice,
Constantly through your life, you could still hear My voice.
All the time all the chances to you I did give,
I'm sorry my child, you've passed up your chance to live."

And as it is appointed unto men once to die, but after this the judgment:

Hebrews 9:27

"Dare to Be a Priest Like Me"

A crucified Christ is what we see,

Saying "Dare to be a Priest like Me."

We see the blood as He hung there,

The crown of thorns seen in His hair.

We see a Christ who suffered and died,

Who was beaten and stabbed in His side.

And on the billboard you can see,

The words "Dare to be a Priest like Me.

But it didn't end in death on the tree,

What about the fight and the victory.

The way Jesus made a show openly,

Of satan and caused him to flee.

The risen Savior in white and full of grace,

With the glory shining about His face.

He has the keys to death, hell and the grave,

He is here to heal, to seek and to save.

To be a priest like Jesus Christ,

Yes it takes surrender and self-sacrifice.

But it also takes living and standing your ground,

And not letting satan push you around.

It's living your life in pure victory,

Exercising your faith and authority.

And a glorified Christ we will see,

Saying "Dare to be a Priest like Me"

For we do not have a High Priest who cannot sympathize with our weaknesses, but was in all points tempted as we are, yet without sin. Hebrews 4:15

"But God!"

It seemed even if people tried to care for me,
No one could help or set me free.
Encouragement was offered for problems each day,
People tried to uplift me when sickness came my way.
Nobody could, But God .
No one could redeem me from the slavery of sin,
No one could renew the right spirit within.
No one could heal my body or ease all my fears,
No one, But God.
I thank God for the day that He made me whole,
He has cleansed me and redeemed my soul.
Even when doctors had given up on me,
He took all my sickness, and now I am free.
No one else cared enough to do this for me,
No one But God.
If you are in sin and you feel you don't have a prayer,
Just know where you are lacking: God is there.
If you are sick in your body and don't know what to do,
If you feel all the world has given up on you.
Everyone But God,
Just turn to Jesus, He'll show you what to do,
Because greater is He that lives inside of you.
If God said it, that is just what He will do,
He's more than the whole world against you.
Stay in His word and He'll lead you each day,
Then with power and boldness you can stand and say.

Now I live my life to please no one, But God!

But God, who is rich in mercy, because of His great love with which He loved us, even when we were dead in trespasses, made us alive together with Christ (by grace you have been saved), and raised us up together, and made us sit together in the heavenly places in Christ Jesus. Ephesians 2:4-6

"Sundays On The Way"

For Jesus Friday was a day of pain, a day resulting in death,
"It is Finished" Jesus said, and then He took His last breath.
He died and was buried, sent to hell as they say.
But the devil somehow forgot, **Sundays On the Way!**

Sunday was the day that made Friday worth it.
Sunday was the day that the plan of God was unearthed.
So when you deal with Friday, and the devil wants to play,
Just look into your situation and know **Sundays on the Way!**

You may be in a Friday situation that has you thinking it's the end,
But just hold on God has promised you no matter what… You win!
You may be in the midst of trouble or filled with dismay,
But Friend we are here to remind you **"Sundays on the Way!"**

For you Sunday is the end of hurt, and the end of all the pain,
Sunday is the beginning of the promise, when life will rise again.
Sunday is encouragement for you, so don't let your faith sway,
Each day in life remember, **your Sundays on the way!**

Looking unto Jesus, the author and finisher of our faith, who for the joy that was set before Him endured the cross.
Hebrews 12:2

Goudeau Gumbo Recipe

Goudeau Gumbo Recipe

Serves 6- 8, (or 4 really hungry)
Prep time 20min, Cook time 1 hour 15 min

Ingredients

Roux

- ½ cup vegetable oil
- ½ cup all-purpose flour

Vegetables

- 1 medium onion, chopped
- 1 green bell pepper, chopped
- 2 celery stalks, chopped
- 3 cloves garlic, minced

Seasoning & Base

- 6 cups seafood or chicken broth
- 1 (14.5 oz) can diced tomatoes (optional)
- 1 cup sliced okra (fresh or frozen)
- 2 bay leaves
- 1 teaspoon paprika
- 1 teaspoon dried thyme
- ½ teaspoon cayenne pepper (optional)
- Salt and black pepper to taste

Seafood

- 1 lb raw shrimp, peeled and deveined
- 8 oz crab meat (lump or claw)
- 8 oz smoked sausage, sliced (Andouille optional)

To Serve

- Cooked white rice
- Chopped green onions (optional)

Instructions

Make the Roux
In a large pot, heat oil over medium heat. Whisk in flour and cook, stirring constantly, until the mixture turns a medium brown color (about 10–15 minutes). Do not rush this step.

Add Vegetables
Stir in onion, bell pepper, and celery. Cook 5 minutes until softened. Add garlic and cook 1 minute more.

Build the Gumbo
Slowly add broth while stirring. Add tomatoes (if using), okra, bay leaves, paprika, thyme, cayenne, salt, and pepper. Bring to a gentle simmer.

Simmer
Reduce heat and simmer uncovered for 30–40 minutes, stirring occasionally.

Add Seafood
Add sausage (if using), shrimp, and crab meat. Simmer 10–15 minutes, or until shrimp are pink and cooked through.

Finish & Serve
Remove bay leaves. Taste and adjust seasoning. Serve hot over rice and garnish with green onions if desired.

~Enjoy Today!

ABOUT THE AUTHOR

Jacqui Hill Goudeau is a born-again Christian who is glad about a decision she made to serve God in 1980. Every day has not been perfect, but she always can run back to a Perfect God. Poetry was always an outlet for her. She never planned to put her thoughts in a book, never wanted to be known for things as simple as her thoughts and visions put into words. But as always, God has a bigger plan for everything!

Wisdom is a huge motivator for her life. Jacqui believes we can ask God for it, and He gives it liberally. Other books include "Departed Friends-Good Grief" that deals with trusting God during hard times. "Getting the Lumps Out of Blended Families" deals with wisdom in our stepfamilies. "The Bear with Black Hair" teaches children organizational skills. She has written over 20 books, and more are in the making.

You can contact Jacqui Goudeau at www.wisdomspeakstoday.com.

www.ingramcontent.com/pod-product-compliance
Lightning Source LLC
LaVergne TN
LVHW051528070426
835507LV00023B/3372